Everybody's Breaking Pieces off of Me

Stress-Relieving Devotions for Women

Susan Lenzkes

BOX 3566 · GRAND RAPIDS, MI 49501

*PUBLISHING BOOKS THAT FEED
THE SOUL WITH THE WORD OF GOD.*

To Dear Herb
husband and friend
Thirty years ago you said that
life with you would be worth at least a
Masters Degree. You were right!
Happy 30th Anniversary.

Special Appreciation to:

Bob DeVries, Carol Holquist, and staff of Discovery House Publishers. Without your loving prayers, touching faith, and patient encouragement, this book would not be here. You found me caught in the stresses and distresses from which this series of books is born, and you believed God for His timing and purposes. Your business is God's business, and it shows.

Julie Link for your sharp editorial skills and graphic artistry. What a joy to work with you again!

Dear friends and family who prayed me through the "schooling" for and the writing of this book. You know I could not have survived, let alone produced, without you. And to my precious Mary Myers. Who but God could have come up with the gift of you?

Library of Congress Cataloging-in-Publication Data
Lenzkes, Susan L.
     Everybody's breaking pieces off of me : stress relieving
     devotions for women / Susan Lenzkes.
          p.   cm.

     ISBN: 0-929239-58-X

     1. Women—Prayer-books and devotions—English. 2. Stress
     (Psychology)—Religious aspects—Christianity—Meditations.
     I. Title.
BV4527.L469   1992
242'.643—dc20   92-21650
                                                                CIP

Discovery House Publishers is affiliated with RBC Ministries,
Grand Rapids, Michigan 49512.

Discovery House books are distributed to the trade by Thomas
Nelson Publishers, Nashville, Tennessee 37214.

Printed in the United States of America

96 97 98 99 00 / CHG / 20 19 18 17 16 15 14 13 12 11 10 9

Introduction

There is a crowded nest of obnoxious baby birds lodged on the beam directly above my bedroom window. At an hour so early it should be scratched from the face of my clock, they begin their "Bugs!-Worms!-Quick!-Hurry!-Me first!-I'm starving!-Can't you see?-Can't you hear?" clamor.

This goes on until the last shred of daylight is gone. And the days are long now. No naptimes. No cease fires.

I worry about their mother. Back and forth. In and out. *Which mouths have I missed? They're all open! All hungry! All the time!* I wonder if she can possibly survive the demands of her responsibilities.

Maybe you feel the same way. If you do, there are at least two of us wondering how we can get through the demands of each day without being pulled apart!

Is there anything in God's Word that will make a difference for us as we "fly back and forth, in and out, trying to maintain a semblance of a nest" in today's stress-filled world?

Join me on a journey of discovery and together we'll find out. But don't expect any monasteries, luxury resorts, or ivory towers along the way! But that's okay; even if life doesn't get easier, we can get better at living it.

Best of all, we'll hear God say, "Enter into my rest."

I could use a little rest. How about you?

Stress Test

Although it happened several years ago, I can still remember the feeling of the moment. It had been the kind of day when you lose track of which interruption is being interrupted. Everyone had been breaking off pieces of me, and someone had just hauled off the last scrap of this wife/mother/friend/churchworker.

I wasn't sure what to do or where to go to find the lost pieces, but I had to do something. I stood in the family room, buttoning myself into my coat.

From his observation point on the couch, my husband asked, "And just where do you think you're going?"

With my arms slicing the air for emphasis, I announced that I didn't know and didn't care, but definitely someplace remote and undemanding. "Everybody expects too much of me!" I concluded, marching to the closet for my purse.

My husband's irritatingly calm voice followed me, "I hope you don't plan to run too far. That car won't make it much beyond forty miles."

Yanking off my coat, I hurled it to the floor and burst into tears. "What am I supposed to do if I can't even run away?"

Realizing that the car wouldn't make it, and neither would I, I stayed home and began a journey that eventually led me to discover why I felt so drained, so spent, so empty. I learned that I am a helpless victim of demanding circumstances only if I *allow* myself to be!

In the midst of life's pressures, problems, and pain I am free to choose attitudes that *produce* stress or *reduce* it. I can *choose* to respond with humor, acceptance, and flexibility. I can act out of a sense of direction that leads to purposeful service.

These are invaluable allies in the fight to become, and remain, whole in a world that tears pieces away from our time, energy, talents, and sanity.

A sense of purpose and trust in God, who knows and loves us, will help us establish priorities. Then we will learn to say "no" without guilt and "yes" without reservation. And finally we will discover the miracle of servant-living when we catch hold of the enormous truth that *people cannot take from us what we freely give away.*

This, then, is how we give ourselves away without coming apart. It is the lesson of the Cross.

The reason my Father loves me is that I lay down my life—only to take it up again. No one takes it from me, but I lay it down of my own accord (John 10:17–18).

Your attitude should be the same as that of Christ Jesus: Who, being in very nature God did not consider equality with God something to be grasped, but made himself nothing, taking the very nature of a servant, being made in human likeness. And being found in appearance as a man he humbled himself and became obedient to death— even death on a cross! (Philippians 2:5–8).

Humble yourselves, therefore, under God's mighty hand, that he may lift you up in due time. Cast all your anxiety on him because he cares for you (1 Peter 5:6–7).

One of Those Days

As you know, we consider blessed those
who have persevered.

JAMES 5:11

However uncharitable the thought, I find myself
hoping that I am not the only one who has been
required to live through days so bad that even Erma
Bombeck wouldn't touch them with a ten-foot
pencil. If I'm the only one, I've evidently been
singled out for abuse in life, because—well, as
humbly as I can say this—my level of expertise in
this arena is hard to beat.

I know, for example, that it doesn't take a
monumental crisis to make "one of those days"—
just a series of common disasters and difficulties
multiplied by the number of people living at your

house. It's like being stoned to death with marbles.

In fact, usually it's the small stuff. The other day, one of our sons was chewing ice and his brother didn't want him to, so he said, "Stop that or I'll deck you," and he didn't so he did.

Add this sort of thing to spills, urgent phone calls, broken dates, skinned knees, frantic searches for keys, a hamster and a cat on the loose, overdue library books, and loud accusations that someone ate (or drank) the last of something that wasn't theirs and they had absolutely no right to do that and who do they think they are anyway…and we have the makings of the kind of day we hope to avoid but never can.

What really bothers me about this kind of day is not that Murphy's Law is having a heyday at my expense. It's that I happen to know that Jesus said, "By this all men will know that you are my disciples if you love one another" (John 13:35).

On days like that, in fact all too often, I am tripping over anything and everything except love.

I'm not naive enough to think that I should be able to get along splendidly at all times, with "never a discouraging word, where the skies are not cloudy all day." Even with only one foot in the real world I understand that in close relationships, things can get crowded. We're bound to bump into one another... and sometimes impatience and anger spill out. And sometimes the people closest to us form a combination that naturally generates sparks.

But if love can't always *keep* peace, it certainly knows how to *make* peace. Love knows the wisdom of a gentle word and a firm hand; the power of an apology and a hug; and the potential of a listening ear that hears and responds to the whimper of need beneath all the shouting.

Love also knows what *not* to do. On "one of those days," active love chooses not to take offense, not to get caught up in the emotional bedlam, not to keep score or flaunt a good memory, not to add to the problem.

But the trouble with such love is, and always has been, that God points His finger at *me* to start the cycle of love—even when I think it makes more sense for Him to make the other guy start, the one creating all the ruckus!

God said that love is patient, kind, gentle, full of hope, persevering, and fail-proof. But He never said love is easy—even when it comes from Him.

May the Lord direct your hearts into God's love and Christ's perseverance (2 Thessalonians 3:5).

Be imitators of God, therefore, as dearly loved children and live a life of love, just as Christ loved us and gave himself up for us as a fragrant offering and sacrifice to God. . . . Live as children of light (for the fruit of the light consists in all goodness, righteousness and truth) and find out what pleases the Lord (Ephesians 5:1–2, 8–10).

May our Lord Jesus Christ himself and God our Father, who loved us and by his grace gave us eternal encouragement and good hope, encourage your hearts and strengthen you in every good deed and word (2 Thessalonians 2:16–17).

The Pressure's On

STRESS IS OUR PERSONAL REACTION TO
PRESSURE.

Some time ago I conducted an informal survey. I
polled a number of people regarding the stress in
their lives. Here—in no particular order—are some
of the things they claim cause stress:

Finances; sibling rivalry; computers; jobs (or
the lack of one); punctuality; pain and illness;
weeds and dirt; clutter; criticism and rejection;
hormones; interruptions; relational difficulties;
telephones (and being "on hold"); final exams;
failure; lousy drivers; red lights (especially when
they're flashing in the rear view mirror!); having to
get up in the morning; wrinkles and gray hairs;

noise; 97 percent humidity; machines, cars (and bodies) that break down; chairing a committee; opinions and expectations; separation; commercials; junk mail; repetitious duties; the neighbor's windchimes; reading the newspaper; clocks; calendars; change; crisis; and a dog, a cat, two birds, and a family of gerbils!

A few people said things like: poor attitudes, a sense of inadequacy, indecision, procrastination, and inflexibility. I give those people credit for both honesty and insight, because I believe they are close to the heart of the matter.

One man responded to my query with a question of his own. "What's the difference between pressure and stress?" he asked.

After a fascinating discussion we decided that all the external annoyances and difficulties which people named—such as noise, illness, interruptions, schedules, and crisis—are pressures. Stress enters the picture when these inevitable problems collide with unhealthy internal reactions—such as bad attitudes and habits, narrow perspective, unrealistic expectations, misconceptions, the need to control, denial, and resistance to change and growth.

When we understand that stress results from

our personal reaction to pressure, we realize how desperately we need to be changed from the inside out. And this adds more stress because we know we are incapable of changing our own hearts.

Gently, God reminds us that the job is His. We are called to trust Him, cooperate with Him, and praise Him for His mighty works. He is able. But are we able to rest... and enjoy Him in the process?

Praise be to the Lord, for he has heard my cry for mercy. The Lord is my strength and my shield; my heart trusts in him, and I am helped. My heart leaps for joy and I will give thanks to him in song. The Lord is the strength of his people, a fortress of salvation for his anointed one. Save your people and bless your inheritance; be their shepherd and carry them forever (Psalm 28:6–9).

The Lord is my shepherd, I shall not be in want. He makes me lie down in green pastures, he leads me beside quiet waters, he restores my soul. He guides me in paths of righteousness for his name's sake.... Surely goodness and love will follow me all the days of my life, and I will dwell in the house of the Lord forever (Psalm 23:1–3, 6).

The Accumulation Situation

"*The truth is,*" *my friend confessed,* "if I dropped dead today, my children would have good reason to hate me for months!"

We had been discussing our perennial plan to get really and truly organized—to somehow win over the multitude of things that twentieth century living collects and deposits in our cupboards, closets, and drawers. We commiserated over the elusiveness of victory and the stress that clutter and disorganization adds to our lives.

My friend was realizing that if she couldn't gain control of the situation, her children would inherit the problem. And there are certain things we would prefer not to have said about us even when we aren't around to hear!

Living simply is not simple. It takes work, discipline, constant choices, defined priorities, and a willingness to say no—to toss out—to give away—and to keep on top of it. It takes a plan and persistence equal to the persistence of junk mail.

If clutter is not part of a scheme to distract us from what is really important, it is at least part of a plan to bury us. It adds to the pressure upon us and cuts into our ability to cope with life's other complexities. It robs us of joy and crowds out time for what is really important.

The good news is that this is one stress we can change. Maybe not all at once. Maybe only one small niche at a time. But progress is measurable here and can be celebrated.

Even better news is that as we clear up and clean out we not only make room for more peace and tranquility, we create time and space for the eternal. More and more we will have opportunity to lovingly touch *people* rather than an endless succession of things.

> *Now about brotherly love we do not need to write to you, for you yourselves have been taught by God to love each other...Yet we urge you, brothers, to do so more and more. Make it your ambition to lead a quiet life, to mind your own business and to work with your hands, just as we told you, so that your daily life may win the respect of outsiders, and so that you will not be dependent on anybody (1 Thessalonians 4:9–12).*

> *May our Lord Jesus Christ himself and God our Father, who loved us and by his grace gave us eternal encouragement and good hope, encourage your hearts and strengthen you in every good deed and word (2 Thessalonians 2:16).*

Learning to Listen

Our frustration must get frustrated with us at
times. It talks and talks, trying to get our attention,
trying to tell us where we're out of balance...where
we're disorganized...where our priorities are not our
own...where we're trying to prove our worth...
where we've settled for external calm in place of
internal peace...where we're covering or com-
pensating for someone else's irresponsibility...
where we're trying to be all things to all people...
where we're chasing impossible ideals... and where

we're tripping over our own bad habits and wrong thinking.

But too often we don't listen. We chastise our frustration as though it were the disease rather than the symptom. So it struggles on, valiantly trying to tell us why the pressure outside us has turned into stress inside us. Endlessly it whispers that our attitudes and expectations may be causing more problems than our circumstances.

And frustration may be only one of the voices clamoring for attention. Exhaustion is groaning its own suggestions. Depression and despair mutter persistent insights. And anger often shouts its declarations over the din of it all.

"How dare they expect so much of me?"

"No matter how hard I try, it's never good enough!"

"Nobody asks what I want!"

"I'll never get caught up!"

"Oh, for just one uninterrupted minute to myself!"

"Whatever I'm doing, I always feel guilty for not doing something else!"

"I can't remember when I last felt rested!"

"What's the use?"

Are we brave enough to stop maligning the messengers and listen to them instead? Faulty beliefs, unrealistic hopes, or deep needs may be revealed in such statements as those above.

Is exhaustion trying to tell us that our worth is not measured by what we produce? Is despair trying to convince us that pleasing everyone won't guarantee their love? Is disappointment trying to tell us that we can't be personally responsible for someone else's happiness? Is anger trying to convince us that conflict is sometimes necessary and good? Is fear trying to tell us that failing doesn't make us a failure? Is dissatisfaction trying to tell us that someone else may be able to do a task as well as we do it? And might frustration itself be reminding us that trying harder won't create a perfect life?

It won't always be pleasant to let the Lord search our hearts and teach us through the voice of our own need. But if we listen carefully we can work with Him to set new, realistic priorities. The actions that result will bring rest and balance to our lives. He knows us and longs to bring us peace. We are safe with Him.

The lamp of the Lord searches the spirit of a man; it searches out his inmost being (Proverbs 20:27).

O Lord, you have searched me and you know me. You know when I sit and when I rise; you perceive my thoughts from afar. You discern my going out and my lying down; you are familiar with all my ways. Before a word is on my tongue you know it completely, O Lord. You hem me in—behind and before; you have laid your hand upon me. Such knowledge is too wonderful for me, too lofty for me to attain. Where can I go from your Spirit? Where can I flee from your presence? Search me, O God, and know my heart; test me and know my anxious thoughts. See if there is any offensive way in me and lead me in the way everlasting (Psalm 139:1–7, 23–24).

When the Wind Stops

GOD TEMPERS THE WIND TO THE SHORN
LAMB.

LAURENCE STERNE

My *clock radio was trying to get my attention*,
pulling me out of another night of exhausted sleep,
annoying me to consciousness with chatter and
laughter. Eventually I realized I was hearing jokes
about the weather from various parts of the
country.

"It's so windy where we live," someone was
saying, "that one day the wind stopped and
everybody fell down!"

My mind awakened just in time to comprehend

this scene, and God broke through to me with its graphic truth. From my prone position I saw a clear picture of my own weary situation.

The winds of trouble and stress had been blowing so long and unrelentingly in my life that I had learned to compensate—to lean into the wind just to stay erect. And when the blast of adversity finally stopped, I fell flat on my face.

There I lay, fatigued from battling my way forward against the gale forces, hurt from the fall, and no longer sure I could walk the narrow way, even if I could summon the energy to struggle to my feet. The old mandate to "pick yourself up, brush yourself off, and start all over again" had lost it's appeal. I couldn't get up. So I found myself praying the most theologically correct prayer anyone in that position could ever pray. I said, "Help, Lord." That was all. Not even an amen.

For the first time in a long time, I began to rest in the knowledge that God knew where I was. He knew, and now I understood afresh that I couldn't stand in my own strength. While flat on my face, I had taken a big step toward finding God's sufficiency.

However, finding God's sufficiency and being

able to appropriate it are two different matters. So I assigned myself a new task: "Stand in the strength of the Lord. Get up and walk! Grab hold of HIS strength!"

But God, who is rich in mercy, quickly pointed out that only He can make us stand. And He does not require us to grasp for His strength. That would be an equally ineffective form of "doing it myself." A weak hand holding onto a strong arm forms a weak bond. It is when strength takes hold of weakness that we can rest, knowing that "underneath are the everlasting arms."

The God of all comfort cares for His hurting, weary children. He waits to hear our cry, waits to lift us out of the pit and hold us close to His heart. When He has nourished and strengthened us, then He will teach us how to walk in the calm as well as in the wind.

Before they call I will answer: while they are still speaking I will hear (Isaiah 65:24).

For this is what the Lord says: "I will extend peace to her like a river…As a mother comforts her child, so will I comfort you" (Isaiah 66:12–13).

I have made you and I will carry you; I will sustain you and I will rescue you...I am God, and there is none like me (Isaiah 46:4, 9).

And the God of all grace, who called you to his eternal glory in Christ, after you have suffered a little while, will himself restore you and make you strong, firm and steadfast. To him be the power for ever and ever. Amen (1 Peter 5:10–11).

If Grace Has a Lap

MANY CHRISTIANS SEEM TO UNDERSTAND
THE CONCEPT OF BEING SAVED BY GRACE,
BUT THEY HAVE MISSED THE CONCEPT OF
BEING SUSTAINED BY GRACE.

JAMES D. MALLORY, JR., *THE KINK AND I*

Almighty God,
  great and
    majestic,
I know that You encircle the
  needs of your children
with the broad embrace of
  eternal solution.
But Abba Father,
  do not leave me
    struggling and unstroked

upon this earth!
If grace has a lap,
  find and hold me there till
all my cries and longings
  snuggle at last into the
Arms of Peace.

All my longings lie open before you, O Lord: my sighing is not hidden from you.... As the deer pants for streams of water, so my soul pants for you, O God. My soul thirsts for God, for the living God. When can I go and meet with God? (Psalm 38:9; 42:1–2).

He tends his flock like a shepherd: He gathers the lambs in his arms and carries them close to his heart; he gently leads those that have young (Isaiah 40:11).

So do not fear, for I am with you; do not be dismayed, for I am your God. I will strengthen you and help you; I will uphold you with my righteous right hand (Isaiah 41:10).

My grace is sufficient for you, for my power is made perfect in weakness (2 Corinthians 12:9).

The Secret of Saying No

If one of the tests for sanity is whether or not "voices" follow us wherever we go, most of us are in a whole lot of trouble. For it seems that on any given day, no matter which way we turn, some voice or another is demanding a chunk of who we are or what we can do.

A better test of sanity would be how we respond to the calls we hear. One of life's greatest challenges will always be in knowing which voice has a right to our time. When do I say yes?

Does every request have equal weight? Do we operate on a first come first served basis? Are we easily persuaded and sidetracked because we have failed to define our priorities, commitments, and giftedness? Or do we have confidence and determination because we understand that by using God's gifts in God's way we will enhance our own lives as well as the lives of those we serve?

Once I was in a committee meeting where someone decided that the best way to fill positions was through bold assumption. "Don't you hear God calling you to be the youth leader?" they asked, pointing at me from across the room.

"No, as a matter of fact, I don't even hear Him whispering!" I said with a smile.

It is easier to respond appropriately when we already are joyously using our gifts. But we also need to take into account our limitations... *real*, not imagined or self-imposed.

The truth is that my health, energy level, or lifestyle demands may be quite different from someone who is doing more than I am and suggesting that I do the same. So it falls to me to continually identify and honor my often shifting boundaries.

I may also find it difficult to say no when I want to please everyone, or be liked or needed, or thought of as wonderful and capable, and so my mouth may say, "Yes, of course I'll do it," while my mind is screaming, "Oh no, not one more thing!"

It is possible that someone, at some time, convinced me by word or example that a truly caring Christian should be able to do it all—and without a ripple of weariness or complaint. Therefore, if a person has a need and I have even an ounce of energy, a smidgeon of talent, or one moment of time, I feel as if I must accommodate the individual because saying no is uncharitable—not "nice."

Besides, if I say no I might feel responsible for their plight... who else will fill that position or do that job?

For all of these flawed reasons and more, a simple no can be very difficult for some of us to say and mean. The word sticks in our throats and chokes us.

But that only happens before we discover the marvelous secret that *inside every carefully thought-out "no" lies a resounding "yes!"*

"No, I can't go shopping right now, because I'm

saying yes to an evening alone with my husband and children."

"No, I won't be able to head up that committee because I'm saying yes to some much needed quiet in my life right now."

We don't need to state our yes aloud. Our no, though small, can stand on its own when said firmly and pleasantly. The yes simply hides there to cancel any false guilt and offer positive direction and purpose to our choice. Yes is a powerful word, both when it is said wholeheartedly and when it is whispered from within a thoughtful no.

We can count on God to give us wisdom concerning all the voices calling for our time and energy. Then we can say yes with joy, and no with grace and confidence.

Whether you turn to the right or to the left, your ears will hear a voice behind you, saying, "This is the way; walk in it" (Isaiah 30:21).

Love the Lord your God, listen to his voice, and hold fast to him. For the Lord is your life (Deuteronomy 30:20).

I will instruct you and teach you in the way you should go; I will counsel you and watch over you.... Rejoice in the Lord and be glad, you righteous; sing, all you who are upright in heart! (Psalm 32:8, 11).

I am always with you; you hold me by my right hand. You guide me with your counsel, and afterward you will take me into glory (Psalm 73:23–24).

Responsible Responsibility

"*I'm not sure I was ever really a kid,*" my friend
confided in me one day. "I think I was born feeling
responsible for helping and fixing everything and
everyone. But you have really helped me to get
over that." She paused, giving me a sideways look.
"You're even better at this than I am, and watching
you has worn me out, so I worked hard to change."

So glad to be of help.

Certain people do seem to be born with—or for

some reason develop—an inflated or misplaced sense of responsibility. Folks count on us. And we appear to do quite well at managing everything and helping everyone. At least for a while. But however it looks on the surface, the result is not responsible responsibility. And it is not healthy.

When my concern for the struggles, problems, and hurts of others weighs me down with the burden of having to fix things, I am the one in need of fixing. While it may appear that I am being pulled apart by the needs of others, a closer look reveals this as an inside job. I am tearing myself apart and giving away great hunks of my time and energy out of a desire to "make it better" and solve other people's problems—or perhaps out of a need to prove myself capable, make myself more comfortable, or be in control.

It is possible to believe that I *am* the only one who can help, or that if I work hard enough I can eventually change other people. Such beliefs wait to be challenged with the truth of God's sovereignty and my limitations!

Responding to needy people around me does not require that I solve their problems. Reaching out does not presume remedy. I am to relieve, not rectify; assist, not alleviate; facilitate, not fix; support, not solve; defend, not deliver. Results are not my responsibility. Loving service is my responsibility.

God is the great Healer, Helper, Defender, Deliverer, Redeemer, and Restorer. He has called His children to be His eyes and ears, His hands and feet, His shoulders and His voice—and to leave the results with Him. What freedom, peace, and joy resides in the truth that God is God, and I am simply a part of His body! I can care and leave the cure to God!

Now you are the body of Christ, and each one of you is a part of it (1Corinthians 12:27).

There are different kinds of service, but the same Lord. There are different kinds of working, but the same God works all of them in all men. Now to each one the manifestation of the Spirit is given for the common good (1 Corinthians 12:5–7).

Each one should use whatever gift he has received to serve others, faithfully administering God's grace in its various forms. If anyone speaks, he should do it as one speaking the very words of God. If anyone serves, he should do it with the strength God provides, so that in all things God may be praised through Jesus Christ. To him be the glory and the power for ever and ever. Amen (1 Peter 4:10–11).

The Place of Peace

"SOMETIMES BEING ALL WRAPPED UP IN
GOD'S WORK BECOMES A SUBSTITUTE FOR
BEING ALL WRAPPED UP IN HIS PRESENCE."

*Octopus schedules
strangle us.
Escalating details,
  demanding deadlines,
    the strain of effort,
  suffocate and isolate.
Oh, to be held,
  rocked,
    freed
in the arms of a hug.
It takes a*

Special Friend
to give such an embrace...
One who said,
"Come unto Me
  all you who labor and are
  heavy laden,
  and I will give you rest."
One called
  Jesus.
Rest in him.

He said to them, "Come with me by yourselves to a quiet place and get some rest" (Mark 6:31).

For anyone who enters God's rest also rests from his own work, just as God did from his. Let us, therefore, make every effort to enter that rest... (Hebrews 4:10–11).

Dancing on His Feet

She took her first steps with great caution, but as her tiny feet learned to cooperate with her brain, she began forging across the floor with her chin thrust forward as though challenging her feet to keep up. And they tried. Though unsteady, they somehow kept going!

Yet her eager feet weren't quite ready for everything she asked of them. When music played, her swaying body demonstrated that it knew instinctively how to respond to rhythm. But no matter what kind of signals her brain sent, those feet could not dance. Each time her feet got into the act she would land smack on her diapered bottom.

Daddy tried to encourage her by dancing in sweeping circles about the room, demonstrating fluid motion. But it was no use. Her will outweighed her skill and over and over she would land at his feet, crying in frustration.

Bending down, Daddy scooped her up and then settled each of her tiny feet atop one of his big shoes. Taking her hands and holding her tall and steady, he slowly danced her about the room until her delighted squeals joined with his laughter. So dancing on Daddy's feet became a daily delight between them.

In my own eagerness to dance through life with grace and joy, my skill seldom equals my will. I hear the music of God's promises, and my spirit yearns to dance. But my feet know only enough to plod forward. Over and over I stumble and fall, crying out in frustration.

Lift me up and place my feet on Your feet, Father, for only You know the dance of joy. Only You are strong and steady. Only You know all the right steps. Only You are full of grace. Thank You for the music.

He set my feet on a rock and gave me a firm place to stand. He put a new song in my mouth, a hymn of praise to our God (Psalm 40:2–3).

Let them praise his name with dancing and make music to him with tambourine and harp. For the Lord takes delight in his people (Psalm 149:3–4).

The Woman

The woman was desperate. And why shouldn't she be? For twelve years she had gone from doctor to doctor, and for twelve years she had gotten sicker and poorer.

When you're in a bad way and unable to find the help you need, there will always be people around with suggestions. They've heard of some great treatment or diet, some exercise or medicine, or some new person in town who's having good results with the friend of a friend.

Well, there did happen to be a new man in town. But nobody claimed He was just "having pretty good results," they said He was doing amazing things—miraculous things! Crippled people who for years had laid in bed or begged by the roadside were dancing with joy. Deaf people began talking and singing His praises. People with all kinds of pain and diseases were healed.

"They say He had a man stand in front of everyone in the synagogue, right in front of the Pharisees and teachers of the law, had him stretch out his shriveled hand, and they all watched it straighten out right in front of their eyes!

"They even say He actually raised a dead man to life, right in the middle of the funeral procession while the grieving mother looked on!

"Our leaders are none too happy about Him, I can tell you. 'Who does He think He is, anyway?' they ask. 'Crowds will follow any lunatic with a good trick,' they say. But *they* sure can't do any of His tricks! They don't much like the way He talks, either.

"But He's interesting! You could just listen all day. Even children follow Him around. They love His stories. But mark my words: There's more to those tales than meets the ear. There is definitely some kind of power in that man. He's not ordinary, even if He does hang around with fishermen and the like. Some people say He's from God…

"You know, He's coming this way. Maybe we could get you close enough to reach Him. The crowds are terrible, but if you could just get hold of some of that power maybe you'd be well again. It costs nothing to try…"

So the woman found herself in the crowd, struggling forward with a growing hope, stumbling and finally stretching toward Him. If only she could touch His cloak, surely she would be healed. And then her fingers brushed His hem. The power flowed into her, warming and healing, startling and thrilling her. She would leave now, quickly, before He saw her.

But He turned and spoke. "Who touched me?" He wanted to know. Amazed, His disciples asked Him which of the hundreds of people jostling and bumping into Him He was referring to? The woman fell to the ground, hiding in fear and awe as she heard Him repeat, "Someone touched me; I know that power has gone out from me" (Luke 8:46).

She trembled, knowing that she had taken what had not been given to her. She had hoped He would fail to notice—that He would let it go. But

He was asking, continuing to look. Why did He have to do this?

Weeping and fearful of what He would do or say to her, she admitted what she had done. Then, with deep love and compassion in His voice, this gentle man of power said, "Daughter, your faith has healed you. Go in peace and be freed from your suffering" (Luke 8:48).

I am in the crowd watching and wondering. What actually happened? Jesus stopped and refused to continue until He found what was taken without His consent. Then He gave it away again.

Was He demonstrating an important truth? Was He warning that sometimes people will recognize the love and power of God in us and reach out in faith, breaking off pieces of our energy, strength, or time? Was He telling us the importance of stopping to give what is so freely given to us? And was He revealing that if we *choose* to give we can keep ourselves from being pulled apart? Does such deliberate generosity help hurting ones finally experience freedom from suffering? Is *this* what our Lord was teaching?

I have set you an example that you should do as I have done for you (John 13:15).

— 48 —

Give, and it will be given to you. A good measure, pressed down, shaken together and running over, will be poured into your lap. For with the measure you use, it will be measured to you.... A student is not above his teacher, but everyone who is fully trained will be like his teacher (Luke 6:38, 40).

Heavenly Approval

"*It must be nice to be Mom,*" our teenage son
commented to his dad one day. "All she has to do is
sleep in, pick up after me, and do a little cooking
now and then."

My husband dutifully passed this assessment on
to me, not even trying to hide his amusement.

There is, I have discovered, an arrogant
blindness that often overcomes young men near the
age of 15. If there is no spontaneous or natural
remission by or about age 21, it is possible the

handicap will be permanent. It is my duty as a mother to pray for him during this dangerous phase of life.

It is also my duty to pray for my own attitude, for it is not good to hold grudges against the ingrates around us.

With all that is required of us in today's world—whether we're parents or just anyone beleaguered by the demands of life—it is easy to fall prey to resentment when we are not properly understood or appreciated. After we've crammed ten pounds of duties into every five-pound day, we're disappointed when people fail to acknowledge all that effort, dedication, and sacrifice!

When we succomb to such disappointment, however, we have given others power over our self-worth. If they fail to affirm us or neglect to applaud our accomplishments, we are frustrated, unfulfilled.

It is time to reassess why we do all that we do. When we begin serving, giving, and doing because these are the right things to do, because they are an appropriate way to spend ourselves and to honor God, we will not be torn apart by the opinions of others.

Naturally it is good when others are happy with

us. But when our focus is right, their understanding and approval delights rather than drives us.

> *Am I now trying to win the approval of men, or of God? Or am I trying to please men? If I were still trying to please men, I would not be a servant of Christ (Galatians 1:10).*

> *Do not work for food that spoils, but for food that endures to eternal life, which the Son of Man will give you. On him God the Father has placed his seal of approval (John 6:27).*

> *And try to learn what is pleasing to the Lord (Ephesians 5:10 RSV).*

A Morning Prayer

MY MOST UNSELFISH ACT MAY BE TO PRAY
FIRST FOR MYSELF.

Jesus, forgive me
for the selfishness of
hurt feelings and
insensitivity
to the needs
of those around me.
Give me your
keen sight and hearing
to know just where to spread
the healing ointment
of your love.
Please provide a supply

just right for today.
And Lord, tie a string
around my heart
reminding me that
this is your day, not mine.

And live a life of love, just as Christ loved us and gave himself up for us as a fragrant offering and sacrifice to God (Ephesians 5:2).

Serve wholeheartedly, as if you were serving the Lord, not men, because you know that the Lord will reward everyone for whatever good he does (Ephesians 6:7–8).

Let us not become weary in doing good, for at the proper time we will reap a harvest if we do not give up. Therefore, as we have opportunity, let us do good to all people, especially to those who belong to the family of believers (Galatians 6:9–10).

The Present

You can only live one day at a time, they say. And
they are right!

Not one of us has more than the present
moment to live—and do—and be. Yet how often
we forfeit today to discontent, depression, and
frustration over what is past or what might lie
ahead.

Stephanie Edwards, a familiar redheaded
television personality here on the West Coast, is a
believer who occasionally struggles with depression.
She offers insight to people who give away the
"now moments"—the only sure gift that time

offers. "People who are depressed," she says, "feel bad about the past, dread the future, and discount the present."

For many, depression is the result of a stressful life, unresolved conflicts, or losses. For some it is the manifestation of a physical problem such as a chemical imbalance or illness. But whatever its cause, and even though it can sometimes be the result of sin or even lead to sin, in its purest form depression is a state, not a sin. And it is never pleasant.

Yet even in the midst of depression, we can ask the Lord to help us find a way to change what we need to change—one small step at a time—and to accept the rest. If we ask our Savior to make us truly content in "whatever state we find ourselves," something begins to change in us and gradually we are able to appreciate God's gift of the present moment.

Stephanie Edwards has found a way to do this. "If we can learn to live life in fifteen minute chunks," she explains, "it forces us to pray constantly, enables us to give worth to this moment's activity, and causes us to see the Lord present—right here, right now."

Learning to live in fifteen-minute chunks may be easier for Stephanie than for the rest of us, since she's used to doing television commercials! But if we try her wisdom, it may help us live a life of eternal significance whatever each day brings to us.

The Lord is near. Do not be anxious about anything, but in everything, by prayer and petition, with thanksgiving, present your requests to God. And the peace of God, which transcends all understanding, will guard your hearts and your minds in Christ Jesus (Philippians 4:5–7).

I have learned to be content whatever the circumstances. I know what it is to be in need, and I know what it is to have plenty. I have learned the secret of being content in any and every situation, whether well fed or hungry, whether living in plenty or in want. I can do everything through him who gives me strength (Philippians 4:11–13).

Search for the Humor

IT BETTER BEFITS A MAN TO LAUGH AT LIFE
THAN TO LAMENT OVER IT.

SENECA

If there were a gold medal for the woman who's
endured the most in unrefined frankness, I'd
probably win it.

One day I was writing in bed when my teenage
son entered the room and sniffed at the long-
stemmed carnation on my dresser, a no-special-
reason gift from my sweet daughter.

"Well, it looks pretty, but it sure doesn't smell
like much," he commented.

Because I can never ignore a chance to teach a
lesson, I responded, "I know what you mean. Those
flowers seem rather like people, don't you think?"

Judging from his surprised look I knew I had his attention, so I went on, "Ever notice how some people look pretty but don't have very fragrant personalities—like this hothouse flower? But have you ever seen one of those spicy little garden-grown carnations? They may be plain looking, but oh, how beautifully fragrant they are, because their beauty comes from within!"

"Right," he agreed enthusiastically. "Just like you, Mom. You don't look like much, but you're really a neat person!"

Swallowing hard, I suggested he might want to learn some tact.

"What's tact?" he asked.

The question didn't surprise me.

"Well," I said thoughtfully, "it might be easier to explain what tact isn't. And to do that, I'll tell you a story about your dad. When we were first married he didn't know much about tact either.

"I used to want your dad to think I was pretty, but he apparently had high standards of beauty back then. He never even hinted that he thought I was beautiful. One night when we were relaxing in front of the fireplace, I cuddled up to him and teased, 'Come on, say you think I'm pretty. You can

do it. Just repeat after me: 'You—are—pretty!'"
And I wheedled and kidded him until finally he
said (in all seriousness, mind you), 'Well, I can't
honestly say I think you're pretty. But I *will* say that
you do pretty well with what you have to work
with!'"

"I get it!" my son burst in. "To be *tactful* he
should have *lied* and said you were pretty!"

Some days a sense of humor is the only thing
that holds me together.

> A *man's [woman's] wisdom gives him [her]
> patience; it is to his [her] glory to overlook an
> offense (Proverbs 19:11).*

> A *cheerful heart is good medicine, but a crushed
> spirit dries up the bones (Proverbs 17:22).*

> *Pleasant words are a honeycomb, sweet to the soul
> and healing to the bones (Proverbs 16:24).*

Haven on Earth

To suggest that we go to people for renewal is like suggesting that we hop from one side of a searing pan to the other. Very often it is from humans that we need relief!

When our burden is people, perhaps we need God's natural refreshment—solitude—in His haven on earth.

> God
> *laces his thickets*
> *with solace,*

soaks his clouds
with cleansing,
arches his skies
with protection,
splashes his flowers
with cheer,
stirs his trees
with a second wind,
buoys his oceans
with assurance,
and heaps his mountains
with hope—
'tis his haven of love,
his hint of heaven.

Ought we—the weary, the worn, the disconsolate
—ignore such generosity?

For the Lord is the great God,
the great King above all gods.
In his hand are the depths of the earth,
and the mountain peaks belong to him.
The sea is his, for he made it,
and his hands formed the dry land.

Come, let us bow down in worship,
  let us kneel before the Lord our Maker;
for he is our God
  and we are the people of his pasture,
the flock under his care (Psalm 95:3–7).

In or Out of Control

I had worked in the peer counseling program for
only a few weeks when I discovered that most of
the people I saw seemed to be struggling with the
same problem. It was not obvious at first. The
stresses and distresses that walked in the door with
each person varied widely in scope and intensity. I
was presented with marital struggles, work-related
dilemmas, problems with abuse, parenting
concerns, low self-esteem, loneliness, loss,
depression, and more.

But after listening carefully, I would inevitably recognize that the person before me was out of control. Oh, there was no unbridled ranting, raving, flailing, or screaming! They hadn't lost control of their emotions and faculties; they were simply no longer in the driver's seat of life.

For some reason, they had allowed their problems to take over, to dominate and dictate, to rob them of choices. Many of them came to realize that of all the difficulties they were experiencing, their worst enemy was the feeling of helplessness.

What a joy it was for us to work together to find that first small step back toward a sense of control. Adversity, pain, and stress are easier to handle when we are no longer at their mercy!

We're going to reign with Christ someday. It is important that we begin now by reigning over our own ability to choose. Perhaps this explains why self-control is a fruit of the Spirit and why God's Word reminds us that there is no law against it.

And we can use the reminder. For deep inside many of us lives the idea that self-control is unlawful—that it is somehow tantamount to being "on the throne of my own life"—that it is in opposition to being controlled by the Spirit.

It is a baffling paradox that we cannot be self-controlled if we are not Spirit-controlled, and yet we cannot be Spirit-controlled if we are not self-controlled. If we are ever going to move into life-changing truth, we need to sort through the confusion.

There are things that we are required to do. The Bible instructs us to *put on* and *take off* certain things, to *let* God do other things, to *present* ourselves, to *give* and *receive*, to *exercise*, to *choose!* These are actions that we must take—actions that require self-control—actions that allow God's Spirit to accomplish His transforming work in our lives.

We know, however, that on our own we cannot do what is right nor please God. His Spirit helps us in our weakness. His Spirit enables us to choose and move in the right direction. It is His work, but we have to take steps and make decisions.

The wise use of self-control means that we repeatedly choose God's control. As we do so, we find ourselves letting go of what is not good for us and reaching out for the riches of our glorious inheritance in Christ Jesus.

Be strong in the grace that is in Christ Jesus (2 Timothy 2:1).

For God did not give us a spirit of timidity, but a spirit of power, of love and of self-discipline (2 Timothy 1:7).

I pray also that the eyes of your heart may be enlightened in order that you may know the hope to which he has called you, the riches of his glorious inheritance in the saints, and his incomparably great power for us who believe (Ephesians 1:18–19).

The Living Example

WISDOM IS THE ACQUIRED ABILITY TO LIVE
LIFE WELL.

DAVID SWARTZ,
DANCING WITH BROKEN BONES

To live life well is to learn to live in the present
and leave our past in the Father's hands. Jesus did
this when, to follow God's will, He left behind His
glory, authority, and power.

We have little more to leave behind than sin,
brokenness, and failure, yet regret has a way of
binding us to our past. We will break free only when
our purpose for moving into the present becomes
the same as Christ's purpose for coming to us.

Jesus came here to do the work of the Father.
This meant He had to become a servant, to lay

aside His heavenly advantage, and to learn to stay in tune with the Father's will one moment at a time.

We are called to do the same—to lay aside our earthly disadvantage and to live moment by moment in complete dependence on the Father's will.

Breaking free from the past and learning to live wisely in the present makes life less complicated, but it does not necessarily mean that it will be more comfortable.

Jesus is our example here too. Life was far from easy for Him. He left the halls of heaven, which reverberated with endless praise and adoration, and landed cold, wet, and squirming on a pile of straw. The government immediately began killing babies, seeking to end His life almost before it began. He and His family became refugees.

He grew up submitting Himself to the teaching and discipline of a man and woman He had created. His preparation for ministry was forty days and nights alone in the desert with no food or water.

He spent the last three years of His life on earth with friends who couldn't grasp who He was or comprehend why He had come. They rarely understood what He was saying or why He said it. He was a constant wanderer. His family once decided He was crazy and tried to take Him back home.

Crowds hounded Him, seeking to use His goodness for their own gain. Church leaders lay in wait to bait and discredit Him. Even His closest friends eventually deserted, denied, and betrayed Him.

The work He had come to do included taking insults, floggings, false accusations, and bearing the most gruesome death imaginable at the hands of pompous, self-righteous men. But He chose to do all of this "for the joy set before Him."

When we are unable to celebrate the present because it is so painful, frustrating, or filled with stress, we need to follow the example of our Lord. We need to reach forward and pull some of the "joy set before us" into our present situation.

As we leave the past behind and borrow liberally from our hope of glory, we find that we can live and rejoice in the present. For God is among us. He is not called "I Was" or "I Will Be," but "I AM." He is here. Now. With us. Whatever is going on in our lives, we can celebrate Him!"

Let us fix our eyes on Jesus, the author and perfecter of our faith, who for the joy set before him endured the cross, scorning its shame, and sat down at the right hand of the throne of God. Consider him who endured such opposition from sinful men, so that you will not grow weary and lose heart (Hebrews 12:2–3).

Anyone who says he is a Christian should live as Christ did (1 John 2:6 TLB).

A student is not above his teacher, nor a servant above his master. It is enough for the student to be like his teacher, and the servant like his master (Matthew 10:24–25).

I have come that they may have life and have it to the full (John 10:10).

Teen Trouble

OH, TO BE ONLY HALF AS WONDERFUL AS MY
CHILD THOUGHT I WAS WHEN HE WAS
SMALL, AND ONLY HALF AS STUPID AS MY
TEEN-AGER NOW THINKS I AM.

REBECCA RICHARDS

Some days should never be recorded, repeated, or
remembered. Take today, for instance. After a
morning of upheaval with my daughter, she
confided that she was in the absolute pits of a
mood. (She could have saved herself the trouble of
making the announcement.)

Then she spent the next hour griping about
everything and anything that has ever touched her
nineteen-year-old world. She said she didn't know
what was the matter with her lately. I have a

permanent crease across my tongue from resisting the urge to tell her!

She finally left for work, and my number-one son must have thought I'd be lonely for disaster, so he proceeded to erupt. He became incensed over some infraction to his personal sense of justice and shoved a bike at his brother, nearly destroying son number two's ability to father succeeding generations.

After tending to the offended, I tried to deal with the offender and got a verbal volley that would knock any mother off her Nikes. An impartial jury surely would have labeled it "mother abuse" and sentenced him to a few years of doing his own cooking and laundry.

So in the middle of this—I mean in the very middle of this scene where I'm debating whether to laugh or to cry because this five-foot-ten-inch kid is exhibiting every characteristic of the "terrible twos" in triplicate—a man called and asked if he had reached the Lenzkes residence...the Susan L. Lenzkes residence.

He had discovered my book *When the Handwriting on the Wall Is in Brown Crayon* in a doctor's waiting room, and he and his wife were so taken by it that they had headed straight for a book store and bought one.

Someone at the bookstore told them where I lived. Then they located my phone number in the directory and called to tell me what a blessing my life was to them! (Who says the Lord's timing isn't perfect!)

Our Lord is faithful. He promised we could pick up snakes with our bare hands, drink deadly poison, *and live with teenagers* (that addition fits nicely, don't you think?) and not be hurt at all!

Do not be far from me, for trouble is near and there is no one to help (Psalm 22:11).

But you are a shield around me, O Lord; you bestow glory on me and lift up my head. To the Lord I cry aloud, and he answers me from his holy hill. Selah. I lie down and sleep; I wake again, because the Lord sustains me…. From the Lord comes deliverance. May your blessing be on your people (Psalm 3:3–5, 8).

A Fountain of Blessing

THE BEST DEFINITION OF REVIVAL IS "TIMES OF REFRESHING…FROM THE PRESENCE OF THE LORD."

J. EDWIN ORR

Sometimes we're so busy going and doing that we don't stop to recognize how weary, dry, and dusty we are. We fail to recognize our great need for refreshment.

My mother wrote of such an experience while she was struggling to know God's presence in the midst of everyday living. She saw her need—and found her answer—in a simple illustration from the God who shows His presence and love in unusual ways. Mother is home now, forever in God's presence, but she left behind "A Fountain of Blessing."

It was a hot day. I had just finished moving the sprinkler close to the back fence when I saw a tiny green hummingbird heading in the direction of the cascading water. I stood motionless, watching in surprise as the bird flew straight into the spray. Instead of whizzing on through as I expected, the bird suddenly reversed its engines and hovered under the umbrella of water.

Ignoring my presence, my little friend leisurely turned from side to side, exposing every portion of his hot and dusty little body to the cool and cleansing water. Finally satisfied, he went back to work, and I went back into the house to ponder my deep emotional reaction to that scene.

I wasn't just watching. I was identifying with the hummingbird's obvious delight as he abandoned himself to the cooling water. His was no accidental encounter. That sharp-eyed little bird recognized the source of blessing and deliberately aimed for it. Instead of rushing on through, he lingered long enough to receive the full blessing of the fountain of water.

God spoke to me through one of the tiniest of his creatures. His presence is here for me the way that fountain of water was for the hummingbird. Just as David proclaims in Psalm 16:11, God was showing me that I only need to recognize and enter into his presence, the fountain of living water, and abide until I experience "fullness of joy!"

—Wilda K. Finefrock, copyright © 1988

Thou wilt make known to me the path of life; In Thy presence is fullness of joy; In Thy right hand there are pleasures forever (Psalm 16:11 NAS).

The Heart of the Matter

Some people worry about being replaced by a computer. Parents never entertain such a worry…they don't even entertain such a hope!

What self-respecting computer would be caught rinsing a diaper in a toilet? No computer has software for such lackluster tasks as mopping spills, folding undershirts, or scrubbing baked-on lasagna. A computer might be of use in repeating such wearisome commands as "close the door," "wash your hands," and "don't hit your sister." But it would have no firm hand to aid the learning process. We might find a computer helpful in organizing lists of duties for ourselves and our children. But computerized lists don't cajole, encourage, or praise.

Computers can say "thank you," but they can't smile when they say it. They can declare "it'll be okay," but they can't wipe away the tears. They can exclaim "you're wonderful," but they cannot confirm it with a warm hug.

The pieces of themselves that mothers and fathers give away day after day might seem wasted. But they are life's daily doses of love wrapped in persistence and patience. No machine can replace that!

> But I said, "I have labored to no purpose; I have spent my strength in vain and for nothing. Yet what is due me is in the Lord's hand, and my reward is with my God" (Isaiah 49:4).

> We always thank God for all of you, mentioning you in our prayers. We continually remember before our God and Father your work produced by

faith, your labor prompted by love, and your endurance inspired by hope in our Lord Jesus Christ (1 Thessalonians 1:2–3).

Flexible Living

STIFFEN YOUR NECK NO MORE.

DEUTERONOMY 10:16 NASB

Many of us are born with a birth defect. The backbone of our character is fused to unyielding rules and regulations. We are rigid in our determination to control life's course and outcome.

We're sure, for example, how people ought to look, behave, and respond. Things have to be done a certain way—our way. We know, too, exactly how a godly marriage should operate; and we're quite familiar with the model of the ideal Christian family—which, of course, we intend to duplicate perfectly.

Then real life sneaks up and whacks us from behind, causing whiplash that nearly breaks our unbending backs and stiff necks. Too many whacks like that and we become paralyzed.

There is a cure however. We can become supple by exercising godly grace and perspective. If we force our muscles of faith, hope, and understanding to stretch, our brittle backbones will become strong and flexible, able to bend with the rhythms of grace yet stand tall and firm against compromise.

All of this requires considerable daily "give." Such give is not a one-time choice but a lifestyle of generosity, spontaneity, and openness to truth.

If I could give just one gift to my children—besides a heart for God—it would be the golden gift of flexibility.

Do not conform any longer to the pattern of this world, but be transformed by the renewing of your mind. Then you will be able to test and approve what God's will is—his good, pleasing and perfect will (Romans 12:2).

And God is able to make all grace abound to you, so that in all things at all times, having all that you need, you will abound in every good work (2 Corinthians 9:8).

Just World Furious

DO NOT BE OVERCOME BY EVIL, BUT OVERCOME EVIL WITH GOOD.

ROMANS 12:21

Every now and then we ought to check the shoulders of our young to see what adult-sized burdens they are carrying—what responsibilities, pain, and fury have they gathered up and hoisted onto their backs?

My youngest son was struggling under a weight that would have staggered even the most fit adult. The heavy realities and injustices of this world were settling in on him, and I might never have known it if he had not been assigned to write a small booklet of poems for one of his grade-school classes.

Among lighthearted poems about himself and his understanding of life I found one called "Just World Furious."

> I'm furious.
> Not just beat-up-someone furious,
> Not go-rip-up-my-room furious,
> Not furious like a man who lost
> His job and he's going to commit
> Harry carry. [sic]
> But just furious with the world
> Because of what it owns.
> Furious because people kill each other,
> Furious because people steal
> Money and commit robberies,
> Furious because I can't do
> Anything about these awful deeds.
>   —Matt Lenzkes. Used by permission.

Furious with the world because of what it owns… Me too, dear son, me too. It is hard to look at the injustices of evil and realize our helplessness to right its wrongs. Opening our eyes wide in this broken, bleeding world and seeing—really seeing—adds to our stress and distress.

But it also suggests important priorities for Christians. For us, and through us, there is hope. We are to be salt—which seasons, purifies, and preserves—and light—which reveals, beckons, and heals. We also are called to spread the Good News that there is One in whom justice dwells—One who overcomes the enemy before the final curtain.

In the meantime, being on stage with evil's closing act brings us both grief and opportunity.

> *Be very careful, then, how you live—not as unwise but as wise, making the most of every opportunity, because the days are evil (Ephesians 5:15–16).*

> *For you were once darkness, but now you are light in the Lord. Live as children of light (for the fruit of the light consists in all goodness, righteousness and truth) and find out what pleases the Lord. Have nothing to do with the fruitless deeds of darkness, but rather expose them (Ephesians 5:8–11).*

> *Finally, be strong in the Lord and in his mighty power. Put on the full armor of God so that you can take your stand against the devil's schemes (Ephesians 6:10–11).*

Stretching Without Breaking

IN HIM ALL THINGS HOLD TOGETHER.

COLOSSIANS 1:17

Certain days are designed for the sole purpose of expanding our coping ability. I did not learn this directly from Scripture. I learned it directly from life.

After one particular morning in which my coping ability was stretched, yanked, and nearly disjointed, I sat down and poured out my woes in a letter to a friend. (I chose this friend because she's single and her frustrations don't include kid stuff, so I get a lot of sympathy from her!)

I wrote:

I was exhausted last night and had a nasty headache coming on, so Herb told me not to get up and fix breakfast…said I was to sleep in. The only way I could have accomplished that was to have been unconscious—which, as I see it now, would have been nice.

With only three children in the house you'd think there would be a mathematical limitation to the possible combinations of fighting pairs, but this morning they exceeded the known possibilities. And when I stepped in to prevent further damage, I only increased the combinations by adding myself to the list!

Everybody was totally innocent, yet everybody was on the attack. Herb had an early flight to Los Angeles, but he told Jeff he'd drive him to school if he was ready by 7 A.M. Jeff wasn't ready (fighting takes time) so Herb had to leave to catch his plane.

He left me with one raging and frantic kid and two possible vehicles with which to transport him (assuming I could hold my throbbing head together and get dressed in time). One vehicle had a flat tire, which no one could explain, and the other had windshield wipers that work only in the sunshine— and of course it was raining.

But I had another idea for a way to get him there. I dressed quickly as frantic announcements of the time came at fifteen-second intervals.

The phone rang. It was Herb. He had barely made it to the airport and his plane was about to leave, but he was wondering how things were going! When I told him, he came up with the same solution I had just hit upon...use the car our friend had left with us.

When I finally got that car warmed up I discovered that the knob labeled "wipers" wouldn't budge the wipers no matter which way I moved it! Jeff ran off in the downpour in an absolute frenzy. (What do they do to kids who are late that triggers such panic?!)

The condition of the house after the kids whirled through it matches the condition of my head. As I write this, ants are marching across the counter feasting on the rich ravages of a kitchen where three kids simply fixed cereal! There goes the phone again.

I recognized the voice at the other end right away because it said, "Mom?" in this I've-got-a-problem-and-it's-all-your-fault-so-you'd-better-help-me-out tone of voice.

"What, Matthew?" I asked in a patient now-I've-got-the-problem-but-what-else-is-new tone of voice.

"You knew I needed valentines today because we're having our party and you didn't get them for me."

"How could I know, Matt? You never told me." I couldn't resist using logic, even on a morning like this.

"Well I have to have them," he said flatly.

So now I have to go out in the rain without a decent car and find cutesy little paper hearts for my son to give to his classmates who probably don't care anyway.

When I get back home—if I ever do—I have to take a shower (though maybe I can skip that after running around in the rain) and then I have to get ready to go speak to thirty pastors on the ministry of counseling. I'll tell you who needs the ministry of counseling about now, old friend!

When we reach the end of our ability to cope, when we are at the absolute end of our rope, it is in Christ that we need to place our hope. For in Him—and only in Him—all things hold together.

He offers peace, rest, and the renewal of our minds, hearts, and coping ability.

> *For in Christ all the fullness of the Deity lives in bodily form, and you have been given fullness in Christ, who is the head over every power and authority....Therefore, as God's chosen people, holy and dearly loved, clothe yourselves with compassion, kindness, humility, gentleness and patience. Bear with each other and forgive whatever grievances you may have against one another. Forgive as the Lord forgave you. And over all these virtues put on love, which binds them all together in perfect unity (Colossians 2:9–10; 3:12–14).*

Choices

Which of us doesn't have a clear mental picture of the "straight and narrow way"?

We begin at the entrance, which, due to the restrictions of holiness, is so small that a person must kneel in surrender to enter. Beyond this gateway, we imagine a neat path that stretches like a slender ribbon of highway—straight and uninterrupted—from here to eternity.

But something bothers me about this neat one-lane road. Real life has more intersections of choice than this rigid image reveals. My perception of the straight-and-narrow needs revision. Instead of being an uninterrupted path, it has many cross-roads. Following Christ takes me across bumpy roads that are regularly interrupted by four-way stops and Y-type intersections. The signposts at these junctions point to glamorous cities and comfortable oases. Some billboards suggest alternative ways to God. Other signs, worn and faded, make the difference between a good route and the best route almost indiscernible. Does it really matter which career, friends, or lifestyle I choose? Does this small moment—this small choice—matter?

It matters. This straight road with its myriad intersections requires the constant map of God's Word as well as unfaltering attention to our faithful guide, Jesus Christ.

The name of the road we travel is "Follow Me." This is our constant choice.

This is what the Lord says: "Stand at the crossroads and look; ask for the ancient paths, ask where the good way is, and walk in it, and you will find rest for your souls" (Jeremiah 6:16).

Obey me, and I will be your God and you will be

*my people. Walk in all the ways I command you,
that it may go well with you (Jeremiah 7:23).*

*Choose my instruction instead of silver, knowledge
rather than choice gold, for wisdom is more precious
than rubies, and nothing you desire can compare
with her (Proverbs 8:10–11).*

No Strings Attached

BEWARE THE ONE WHO SERVES HIS OWN
NEEDS BY CLAIMING TO SERVE YOURS.

It was one of those rare, luxurious wake-up-at-
your-own-pace Saturday mornings. My husband and
I were taking full advantage, stretching and purring
like cats on a hearth, when our fourteen-year-old son
joined us, landing on top of his dad's back.

Eventually I heard my husband say, and it was
quite obviously directed to his piggy-backer, "A cup
of coffee sure does sound good!"

"Sure does!" I agreed enthusiastically.

Our son began a loud protest. "Oh, no, you
guys are just trying to put a guilt trip on me! I don't
want to make you coffee!"

"Well, we were just saying it would be *good*," his dad reiterated.

"Sounds pretty straightforward to me," I observed. "Besides," I went on, beginning to wake up to the fun of it, "didn't Jesus say it's more blessed to give than to receive? We're just trying to get you *blessed!*"

"That's right," my husband joined in, "we're only doing this for *you!*"

"All right, all right, I'll get your coffee!" he yelled, jumping up and rushing out. You guys are the *major* guilt-trippers!"

Wide-eyed with feigned innocence, my husband and I looked at one another, asking how on earth he could think such a thing. Then we giggled—two successful conspirators.

Fun stuff—when it's deliberately light-hearted and everyone's playing the game. Trouble is, real manipulation is accomplished subtly, regularly, and with serious consequence.

Manipulation, well done, gets us what we want, but at the expense of another person's freedom.

"You *owe* me…,"

"But haven't you always *said*…,"

"How *could* you, after all I've done…,"

"Everyone *else* knows that...,"
"God's Word says you *have* to...,"
"If you really *loved* me...,"
"Don't you *trust* me...,"
"Someday when I'm *gone*...,"
and so on.

Sometimes we don't even need words. A wounded look, a sigh of disappointment, or an authoritarian glare serve just as well.

To be completely honest, we have to admit that manipulation is a relational cancer. And when we practice such coercion, we are diseased people.

Another honest look reveals that those who allow themselves to *be* manipulated are feeding the cancer—contributing to the sickness. Good reason to practice a firm "no" or learn to withdraw from the clutches of a conniver—whether acquaintance, family member, or friend.

At great personal expense, God gifted us with the freedom of choice. The bold manipulator dares to live out this message: "The Lord giveth, *I* take away!"

You, my brothers [and sisters] were called to be free. But do not use your freedom to indulge the sinful nature; rather, serve one another in love. The entire law is summed up in a single command: "Love your neighbor as yourself." If you keep on biting and devouring each other, watch out or you will be destroyed by each other.... But the fruit of the Spirit is love, joy, peace, patience, kindness, goodness, faithfulness, gentleness and self-control. Against such things there is no law (Galatians 5:13–15, 22–23).

Climbing Higher

"*Parenting is a high and holy calling,*" came the pronouncement from the pulpit.

"High and holy calling, indeed," I muttered, slumping back in my seat. "High, because they have us climbing the walls half the time, and holy because they use us for target practice the other half!"

I had, in fact, arrived at that service late—just in time to hear the choir sing without me— precisely because of my parental calling. My youngest had been practicing outrageous defiance during an assumed "safety period"—he knew Mom was scurrying to get to choir on time. But he came to a new understanding of my priorities when I turned the car toward home and he realized that a private lesson was about to be impressed upon his, uh, mind.

It doesn't help to romanticize the rugged call of parenting. It does help to pray that we stay tough and tender and that we learn and grow along with our children.

When we do find ourselves as high as the ceiling, it helps to look still higher—until we have a perspective as high and holy as our Lord's.

Endure hardship as discipline; God is treating you as sons. For what son is not disciplined by his father? If you are not disciplined (and everyone undergoes discipline), then you are illegitimate children and not true sons. Moreover we have all had human fathers who disciplined us and we respected them for it. How much more should we submit to the Father of our spirits and live! Our fathers disciplined us for a little while as they thought best; but God disciplines us for our good that we may share in his holiness. No discipline seems pleasant at the time, but painful. Later on, however, it produces a harvest of righteousness and peace for those who have been trained by it. Therefore, strengthen your feeble arms and weak knees (Hebrews 12:7–12).

An Emotional Riddle

THE HEART HAS ITS REASONS WHICH
REASON DOES NOT UNDERSTAND.
BLAISE PASCAL

What has the power to make small things large and large things small, shy people bold and bold people shy, or bright days dark and dark days bright? A mood!

Moods are colored glasses through which we look at our world.

The other morning I got out of bed to an unbelievably gorgeous, sunny day. My mood, however, perhaps in reaction to protracted physical pain, clouded things over considerably.

Today, on the other hand, the canyons outside my window are being swept with huge brooms of wind-driven rain, and the sky is depression gray. But my inner sunshine is back, so I'm free to enjoy the rain.

Through these same tinted spectacles we view ourselves. Sometimes when I'm about to speak at a conference or retreat, I experience a wonderful feeling of confidence and ease—even eagerness. Other times, even though I've prepared, prayed, and committed myself in exactly the same way, I fight jitters, concern, and the urge to say, "Why me, Lord? I have nothing worth saying!"

Some moods are like a magnifying lens, making small irritations appear large and causing over-sized reactions to ordinary situations. Take, for example, the jumble of bookbags, sweatshirts, sportsgear, and shoes that inevitably lands when my boys arrive home. If I am in a certain unfortunate mood, this ordinary clutter becomes a direct and personal attack on my need for order.

So instead of saying, "All right, guys, to your rooms with this stuff," I say…well, never mind what I say! They wish I had spared them, too!

Ranging from wonderful to difficult to downright depressive, moods are a natural response to all that affects us from without and from within—and some days we can't even pinpoint their source!

We can find comfort in the truth that moods can be managed, lived with in wisdom, and even used positively when they are submitted to the One who alone knows how to color our world and enable us to see it clearly.

You will keep in perfect peace him whose mind is steadfast because he trusts in you. Trust in the Lord forever, for the Lord, the Lord, is the Rock eternal (Isaiah 26:3–4).

Therefore everyone who hears these words of mine and puts them into practice is like a wise man who built his house on the rock. The rain came down, the streams rose, and the winds blew and beat against that house; yet it did not fall, because it had its foundation on the rock (Matthew 7:24–25).

Night Class in Obedience

WE MUST OBEY GOD RATHER THAN MEN!

ACTS 5:29

It was a bad dream and I awoke in tears. The dream began with a phone call from a friend announcing his imminent arrival. For whatever reason, the house was in shambles. I hung up the phone and quickly announced a plan of action, assigning each family member a separate area of work.

Though all voices assented to the plan, I noticed, as I whirled by doing my own task, that my son still sat calmly reading the paper.

"Hurry!" I called out. "We don't have much time. He'll be here soon!"

"Oh sure, Mom," he replied pleasantly, and then casually settled back with the sports page.

A rage of protest welled up in me at his practiced, polite indifference. It was then that I awakened both my husband and myself as my frustration erupted into sobbing.

The next morning I was haunted by my inordinate response to such an ordinary aggravation. No amount of surmising or analyzing brought a satisfactory explanation.

Finally, preparing myself to learn some new truth about either me or my son, I prayed, "Lord, if there's something I need to understand from this, teach me."

Suddenly I heard my Heavenly Father call out, "Children, time is short! I have jobs for each of you!"

I heard myself give assent to His instructions. Then I watched as I went about my own business.

"Hurry," He called when He found me idle, "He will be here soon. I have given you a job to do which I've assigned to no one else."

And I responded, pleasantly enough, "Of course, Father," and then went back to my reading.

I sat stunned at this revelation. Then He went

on, "Sometimes you even tell me, most sincerely, that you *love* me—right before you go back to your reading. How would you have felt if your son had done that?"

He continued, "My child, it is even worse than that. Your son was only reading the sports page. How deep would your hurt have been if, instead, he were re-reading a very familiar and well-understood list of your urgent instructions for him—searching them for deeper meaning or commenting on their style, form, or accuracy?

"Suppose that when you called out, 'Hurry, there is much to do. Time is short for he is coming!' your child arose but walked right on by the mess and got together with his brother to study your instructions? And suppose he expected you to reward him for this behavior?"

"Dear child, listen and truly learn; all the deeper meaning, all peace, and all reward is found in simple obedience."

The word is very near you; it is in your mouth and in your heart so you may obey it (Deuteronomy 30:14).

Do not merely listen to the word, and so deceive yourselves. Do what it says. Anyone who listens to the word but does not do what it says is like a man who looks at his face in a mirror and, after looking at himself, goes away and immediately forgets what he looks like. But the man who looks intently into the perfect law that gives freedom, and continues to do this, not forgetting what he has heard, but doing it—he will be blessed in what he does (James 1:22–25).

Jesus replied, "If anyone loves me, he will obey my teaching. My Father will love him, and we will come to him and make our home with him" (John 14:23).

Force Fitting

*No one wants to think
  he's got it wrong—
That all the patches
Went on backwards,
All the layers,
  upside down.
It's harder
When you're sitting
  in the middle,
Trying to smooth*

the pieces,
Fit it all together,
Make it come out even
  at the edges.
Somehow the grand design
  gets lost,
And you end up sewing
Anything that meets.
  —Judith Deem Dupree,
    Going Home, copyright © 1984

Surely you desire truth in the inner parts; you teach me wisdom in the inmost place. Cleanse me with hyssop, and I will be clean; wash me, and I will be whiter than snow (Psalm 51:6–7).

If you call out for insight and cry aloud for understanding, and if you look for it as for silver and search for it as for hidden treasure, then you will understand the fear of the Lord and find the knowledge of God. For the Lord gives wisdom, and from his mouth come knowledge and understanding. He holds victory in store for the upright.... Then you will understand what is right and just and fair—every good path. For wisdom

*will enter your heart, and knowledge will be
pleasant to your soul. Discretion will protect you,
and understanding will guard you (Proverbs 2:3–7,
9–11).*

A Circle of Rest

DROP THY STILL DEWS OF QUIETNESS TILL
ALL OUR STRIVING CEASE...

JOHN GREENLEAF WHITTIER

Teach me, Lord!
I know I need to learn a lesson
of restraint,
of priorities,
or I would never be this tired.
But teach me, Father,
not from the distance of heaven
nor from behind a pulpit or podium,
but from within your embrace.
Teach me your tender love and leading
as I rest on your
mighty shoulder,

then whisper to me
what I keep forgetting...
I must rest within your arms
constantly
to rest within your will.

Find rest, O my soul, in God alone; my hope comes from him (Psalm 62:5).

Come to me, all you who are weary and burdened, and I will give you rest. Take my yoke upon you and learn from me, for I am gentle and humble in heart, and you will find rest for your souls. For my yoke is easy and my burden is light (Matthew 11:28–30).

Duty Nags

DUTY CALLS LOUDEST TO THE HARD OF
HEARING.

I know that my son, the one who hates to pull
weeds, has never yet read the entire Bible. If he had
he would have quoted Ecclesiastes 2:17 by now,
claiming biblical backing for the stance that "work
done under the sun is grievous to me. All of it is
meaningless, a chasing after the wind."

I sympathize with him. What could be more
meaningless than repetitious, lackluster tasks with
no challenge and no end in sight? Surely, we were
made for better things!

Yet such duties, when ignored, have a way of
doubling themselves.

Take my refrigerator, for instance. I save things—bits of this and that—leftovers that a frugal conscience will not allow me to toss out, no matter how small. Yet, once time has done her hoary duty, my conscience is the first to suggest where such garbage belongs. By then, however, the rest of me is resisting involvement.

Cleaning the refrigerator is grievous to me. When I don't clean it, it is grievous to my husband. At times he has even tackled the job himself. At other times he has waited and won. The other day he approached the whole problem differently.

I came home to find an open container with a note attached. The contents were awesome looking—surely high-yield gain in any penicillin lab.

"Success again!" the note exclaimed. "Now, after *many* tests, we have, once again, demonstrated to the world and our outspoken critics that green things can be grown successfully in cold, dark places. Hereafter the need to grow green things in the refrigerator is no longer required. Chief Scientist."

I appreciated the humor. And I saw truth growing among the green things.

One who is slack in his work is brother to one who destroys (Proverbs 18:9).

He who works his land will have abundant food, but the one who chases fantasies will have his fill of poverty. A faithful man will be richly blessed (Proverbs 28:19–20).

From heaven the Lord looks down and sees all mankind; from his dwelling place he watches all who live on earth—he who forms the hearts of all, who considers everything they do.... My eyes will be on the faithful in the land, that they may dwell with me (Psalm 33:13–15; 101:6).

Fighting the Real Battles

FIGHTING THE GOOD FIGHT REQUIRES
FIGHTING THE RIGHT FIGHT.

If you're a kitten and you're honing your jungle instincts, everything is suspect. Life requires a constant state of alert. One must be primed, nimble-footed, and ready to bristle and lunge at a moment's notice, for things are never as harmless as they seem.

Fully convinced of this, our kitten spied me reading a book on the living room couch one day and launched a surprise attack from the stairs above. (It took my heart only five or ten minutes to resume its normal rhythm!) Later, he caught my toe moving, pounced on it, and wrestled it into submission.

And what about lethal inanimate objects? Above all, never trust them! They're only playing possum. One day our kitten bravely stalked and killed one of my most amenable, non-threatening houseslippers. He didn't even seem to notice that it never fought back. Victory must be in the eye of the aggressor!

I wonder how many battles I've won that weren't a real fight in the first place? How much of my energy have I spent unnecessarily? How many times have I stalked the corpse of some forgiven sin, wrestled valiantly, and then proudly claimed victory?

Perhaps I've pussy-footed around imaginary threats, bristling at everything. Have I pounced on people who meant me no harm? Do I have a trophy room full of dead houseslippers?

Have I backed away from life's realities, circled cautiously, then attacked with the claws of idealism?

Has every new movement, anything unfamiliar, seemed a danger to me—something to be disarmed?

Am I neurotically prowling through life playing jungle cat in the midst of real warfare?

When will I learn who my real enemy is? When will I learn the difference between real and imaginary battles?

For our struggle is not against flesh and blood, but against the rulers, against the authorities, against the powers of this dark world and against the spiritual forces of evil in the heavenly realms. Therefore put on the full armor of God, so that when the day of evil comes, you may be able to stand your ground, and after you have done everything to stand. Stand firm then, with the belt of truth buckled around your waist, with the breastplate of righteousness in place, and with your feet fitted with the readiness that comes from the gospel of peace. In addition to all this, take up the shield of faith, with which you can extinguish all the flaming arrows of the evil one. Take the helmet of salvation and the sword of the Spirit, which is the word of God. And pray in the Spirit on all occasions with all kinds of prayers and requests. With this in mind, be alert and always keep on praying for all the saints (Ephesians 6:12–18).

Feed Thy Soul

O MY SOUL... FORGET NOT ALL HIS BENEFITS.

PSALM 103:2

If I were required to climb onto an examination table right now and present myself along with my schedule, expectations, exhaustion, and stress to wisdom's scrutiny, I might prefer to skip the diagnosis. But within wisdom lies hope and help, so I listen to the doctor:

"Your coping systems are moderately to severely impaired," comes the solemn pronouncement. "You're suffering from chronic time deficiency syndrome, pernicious energy anemia, dehydrated patience and creativity levels, and some degree of residual despair.

"But perhaps most serious of all, because this

affects your overall balance and health, you are dangerously deficient in basic nourishment of the soul.

"Take time to get to know yourself and your needs. Realize that you were created in the image of God who is lavish with beauty. He distributes it from the most inaccessible mountain top to the deepest part of the sea. All around you, flowers bloom and die in bursts of fragrant delight, soft spun clouds sail by unnoticed, a child waits to laugh with you, friends stretch out their hands, and joy sits untasted, unclaimed.

"While you struggle amid poverty of time and energy, your limitless Creator yearns for you to enjoy the refreshing beauty of Who He is and to savor His generous gifts. The soul renewed better understands how to walk and not faint.

"Here, then, is your prescription for recovery:

*If thou of fortune be
bereft
And in thy store there
be but left
Two loaves, sell one
and with the dole*

Buy hyacinths to
feed thy soul.
    —James Terry White

Praise the Lord, O my soul; all my inmost being,
praise his holy name. Praise the Lord, O my soul,
and forget not all his benefits…who redeems your
life from the pit and crowns you with love and
compassion, who satisfies your desires with good
things so that your youth is renewed like the eagle's
(Psalm 103:1–2, 4–5).

Today Is Tomorrow

IS NOT WHAT I SHALL BE CAPABLE OF
TOMORROW CONTAINED IN WHAT I AM
TODAY?

PAUL TOURNIER

Let's get started on tomorrow.
Let's reach out
through each day's clouds and sunshine and
* reshape our stresses,*
* sharpen our priorities,*
* learn our lessons,*
* touch our purpose,*
* taste our potential,*
* and claim our inheritance in Christ.*
Let's get started on tomorrow by
living fully and gratefully

this day.
Each day, well lived,
peeks around the curtain and effortlessly
pre-arranges tomorrow.

But seek first his kingdom and his righteousness, and all these things will be given to you as well. Therefore do not worry about tomorrow, for tomorrow will worry about itself. Each day has enough trouble of its own (Matthew 6:34).

Be joyful always; pray continually; give thanks in all circumstances, for this is God's will for you in Christ Jesus…. May God himself, the God of peace, sanctify you through and through. May your whole spirit, soul and body be kept blameless at the coming of our Lord Jesus Christ. The one who calls you is faithful and he will do it (1 Thessalonians 5:16–18, 23–24).

Putting the Pieces Together

GOD IS ALWAYS WORKING WITH THE END
RESULT IN FULL VIEW.

Sorting through the rich variety at His fingertips,
the Master quilt-maker carefully arranges the pieces
of cloth. Sometimes He smiles as He works.
Sometimes He smiles through tears. Now and then
He holds the fabric tenderly for a long time before
placing it.

Reaching for a large swatch, He traces the
bright pattern of memories woven into its design,
then smooths it into place beside a costly scrap of
deep blue, which is dapple-stained with grief's tears.

Next to that He lays a dark bit of doubt, then a shimmering strip of hope, followed by a ragged fragment of frustrating demands, encircled by lustrous snips of praise. Can He possibly know what He's doing? Near the center He places a remnant from a well-worn garment torn from the point where the knee bends. All of this He borders with bands of white from a seamless robe.

Finally, through the eye of His needle, He inserts a golden thread of *trust*—gathered and saved with great joy. Then He begins stitching the pieces into place. The needle pricks His hand, but He continues working, leaving traces of red at each cross-stitch.

A pattern emerges; an incredibly wonderful blend of color and design. The *re*-Creator is at work, putting the pieces of my life together— creating beauty from brokenness.

He continues as I supply the thread.

For we are God's workmanship, created in Christ Jesus (Ephesians 2:10).

I praise you because I am fearfully and wonderfully made; your works are wonderful, I know that full well. My frame was not hidden from you when I was made in the secret place. When I was woven together in the depth of the earth, your eyes saw my unformed body. All the days ordained for me were written in your book before one of them came to be (Psalm 139:14–16).

Great is the Lord and most worthy of praise; his greatness no one can fathom. One generation will commend your works to another; they will tell of your mighty acts. They will speak of the glorious splendor of your majesty. and I will meditate on your wonderful works (Psalm 145:3–5).

That Final Piece

IT IS A TRAGEDY OF THE CONTEMPORARY
CHURCH THAT ALL TOO MANY CHRISTIANS
LIVE IN SPIRITUAL POVERTY, COMPLETELY
UNAWARE OF THE RICHES THAT LIE SO CLOSE
AT HAND, JUST WAITING TO BE TAPPED.

RON LEE DAVIS,

BECOMING A WHOLE PERSON

IN A BROKEN WORLD

For so long
I clung to that
  last
    bit
      of
        self
hoarding fragile resources,
heeding frantic warnings:
Use sparingly,

for when your crumb is gone
you will be
finished.
How could I have known?
Fear's final effort
held the
chink in the wall
between
my meager supply
and the flood of
God's
great
wealth!

[You are] sorrowful, yet always rejoicing; poor, yet making many rich; having nothing, and yet possessing everything (2 Corinthians 6:10).

The glorious riches of this mystery is Christ in you, the hope of glory (Colossians 1:27).

Note to the Reader

The publisher invites you to share your response to the message of this book by writing Discovery House Publishers, Box 3566, Grand Rapids, MI 49501, USA. For information about other Discovery House books, music, or videos, contact us at the same address or call 1-800-653-8333. Find us on the Internet at http://www.dhp.org/ or send E-mail to books@dhp.org.